Contents

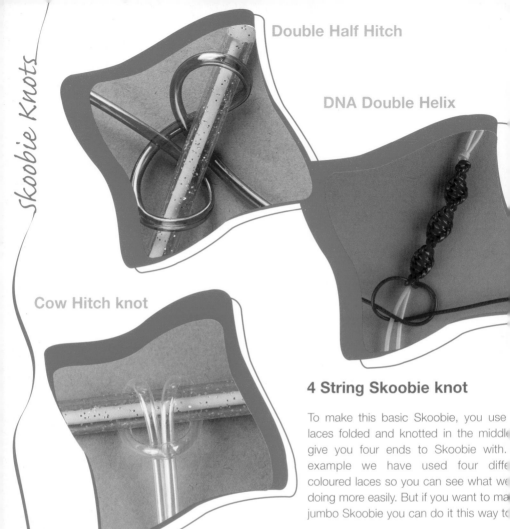

Double Half Hitch

DNA Double Helix

Cow Hitch knot

4 String Skoobie knot

To make this basic Skoobie, you use
laces folded and knotted in the middle
give you four ends to Skoobie with.
example we have used four diffe
coloured laces so you can see what we
doing more easily. But if you want to ma
jumbo Skoobie you can do it this way to

Skoobie Knots

For those of you just getting into the Skoobie
phenomenon here are the Skoobie Knots.
Once you have learned how to start the
basic Skoobie knot you will only be limited by
your imagination.

The main knots that we have used throughout
this book are the Double Half Hitch, Cow
Hitch, 4 String Skoobie and the Weave.
Another useful knot you may use is the
Double Helix.

Good luck and welcome to the wonderful
world of Skoobies!

1) Take 4 different coloured laces (red, ora
   white and yellow), take all 4 ends and
   them all together and tie one big knot to
   all the laces together.
2) Hold this knot in one hand, with the o
   hand spread out the laces so they all
   out and form a cross (+) with the knot in
   middle. The colours following around are
   orange, white and yellow.
3 - 4) Now go round in a circle starting with
   put the red lace over the orange lace
   place it over the white lace, take the w
   lace and put this over the yellow lace.
   thread the yellow lace over the red lace
   under the orange lace.

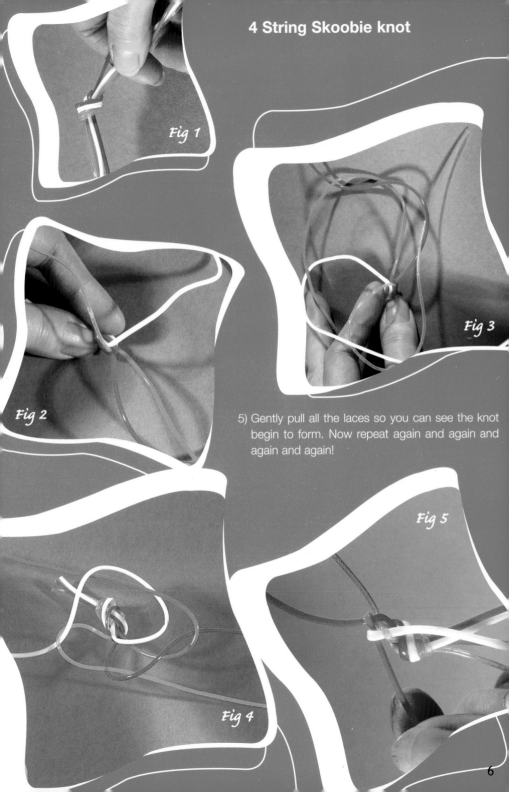

4 String Skoobie knot

Fig 1

Fig 2

Fig 3

Fig 4

Fig 5

5) Gently pull all the laces so you can see the knot begin to form. Now repeat again and again and again and again!

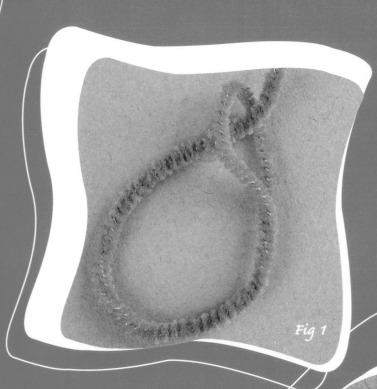

Fig 1

Fig 2

The Weave

1 - 2) Make a circle with the pipe cleaner.

3) Attach a lace to the pipe cleaner loop using a Cow Hitch knot at the top. Attach it to the opposite side using a double half hitch so that one lace is much longer than the other.

4) Use the long length of lace to weave in between the outside pipe cleaner and the middle double strings.

5) Cut off excess lace.

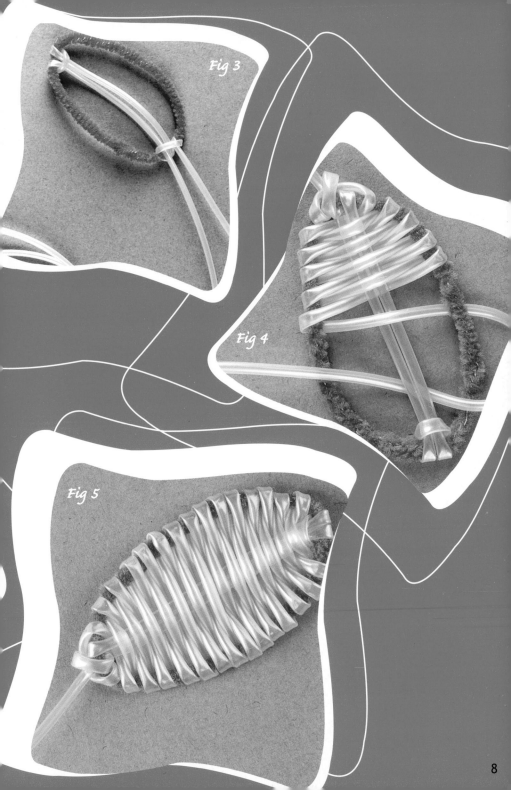

Fig 3

Fig 4

Fig 5

8

Heart

1 - 2) Take 4 separate red laces and knot them together in the middle. You will be working with one half the length of the laces to begin with.

3) Loop the laces to form a round Skoobie and continue until you have made a Skoobie about 10 cm long.

4 - 5) Undo the knot in the middle of the laces and start to use the other half of the laces. Make the right angle by pushing two laces down and across the side of the made Skoobie so you have all four laces sticking out in one direction to the side of the Skoobie. Continue to Skoobie for another 10 cm.

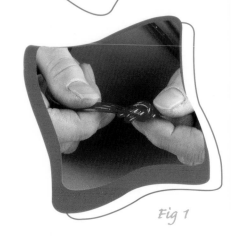

Fig 1

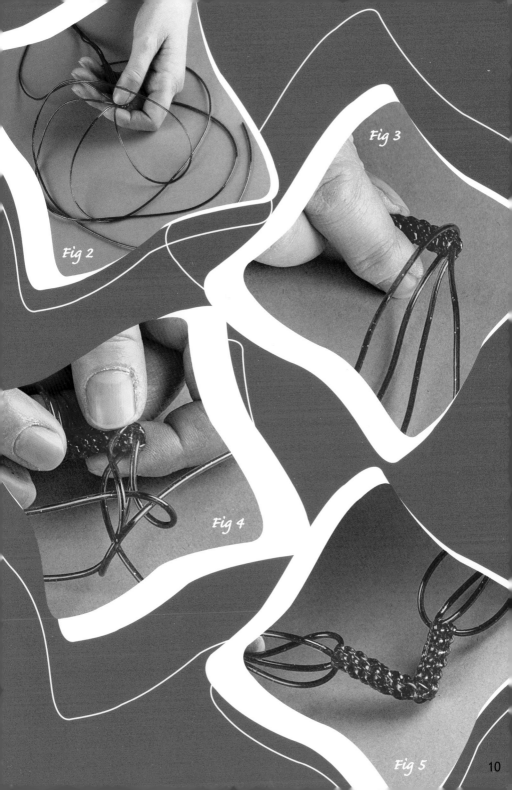

Fig 2

Fig 3

Fig 4

Fig 5

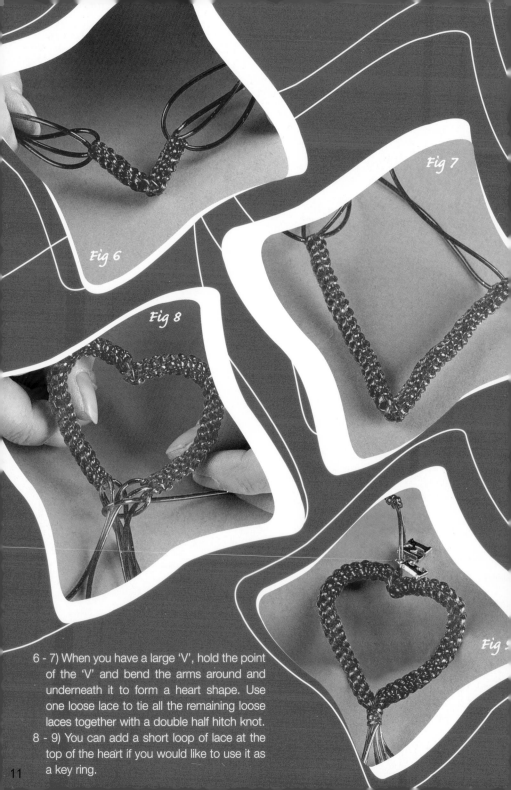

Fig 7

Fig 6

Fig 8

Fig 9

6 - 7) When you have a large 'V', hold the point of the 'V' and bend the arms around and underneath it to form a heart shape. Use one loose lace to tie all the remaining loose laces together with a double half hitch knot.

8 - 9) You can add a short loop of lace at the top of the heart if you would like to use it as a key ring.

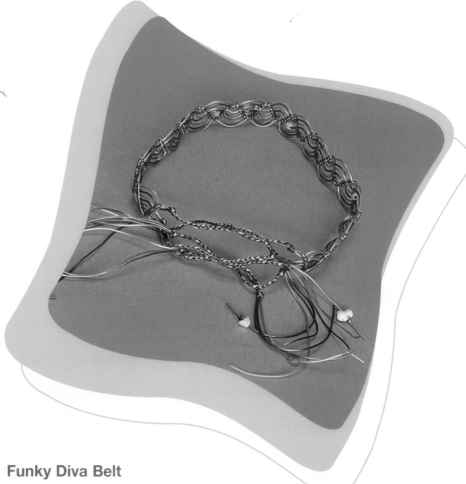

Funky Diva Belt

1 - 3) Use 8 long laces. Take the left outside lace (purple) for your knotting string. Using a red lace use a Double Half Hitch knot to attach it to the purple knotting lace.

4 - 5) Holding purple knotting lace to the right. Repeat with a purple lace to the purple knotting string, then another red and continue alternating the colour each time.

6 - 7) When all laces have been knotted onto the knotting string it is time to turn and work back in the opposite direction. This is done by holding the knotting lace to the left and reversing the Double Half Hitch knot (see diagram 7) Use the alternating coloured laces in the reverse order to how they were used the first time.

Fig 1

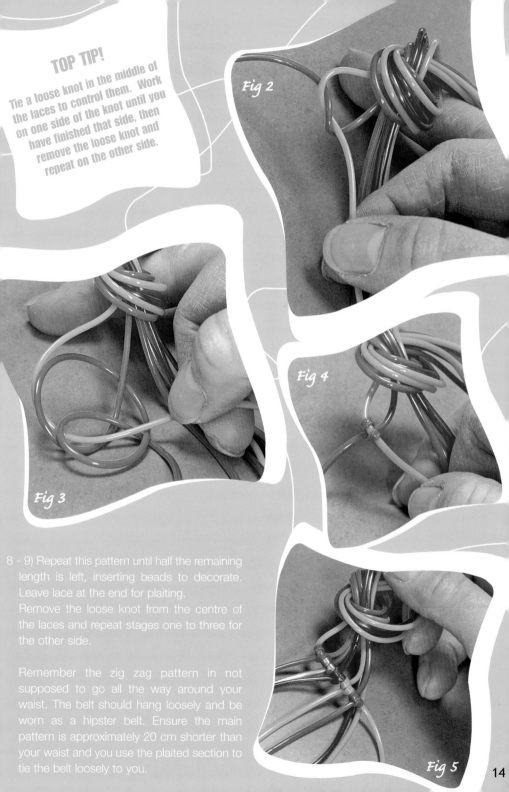

TOP TIP!

Tie a loose knot in the middle of the laces to control them. Work on one side of the knot until you have finished that side, then remove the loose knot and repeat on the other side.

Fig 2

Fig 4

Fig 3

8 - 9) Repeat this pattern until half the remaining length is left, inserting beads to decorate. Leave lace at the end for plaiting.

Remove the loose knot from the centre of the laces and repeat stages one to three for the other side.

Remember the zig zag pattern in not supposed to go all the way around your waist. The belt should hang loosely and be worn as a hipster belt. Ensure the main pattern is approximately 20 cm shorter than your waist and you use the plaited section to tie the belt loosely to you.

Fig 5

14

Take the outside three laces, knot and plait. To the middle two add an extra lace when you knot so you have three for the plait. Make the plaits about 15 cm then knot.

11) Make the remaining loose laces different lengths, add beads for decoration, and knot.

Now you can make our Funky Diva Belt you can make a matching set of bracelets, necklaces and chokers. Take a careful look at our choker which was made with 5 strings, the box knot and some trinkets for added pizzazz and see if you can recreate it, then make some matching bracelets and anklets. You could even mount a mini version on a hair clip. Good Luck.

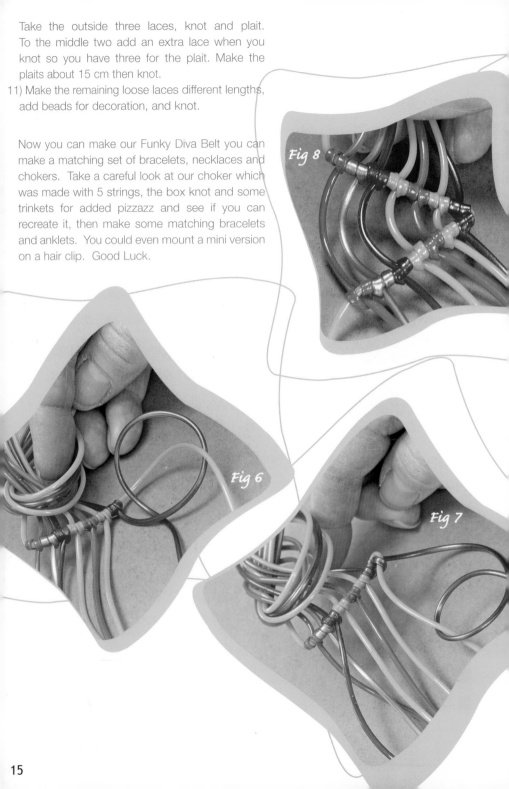

Fig 8

Fig 6

Fig 7

Fig 9

Fig 10

Fig 11

Matching Funky
Diva Bracelet

Aeroplane

We have made a large Aeroplane by using a thick lace for the planes body. If you want to make a smaller version, simply use a normal sized lace. If you are feeling really adventurous try making the planes body by doubling up and knotting eight strings in the same way you would use four.

1) Make the body using the standard·round Skoobie knot, for about 2-3cm.

2 - 3) For each layer after that, thread one lace through the knot so it lays across the body and sticks out equally either side. This is for making the wings. You will need to do this 7 times.

Fig 1

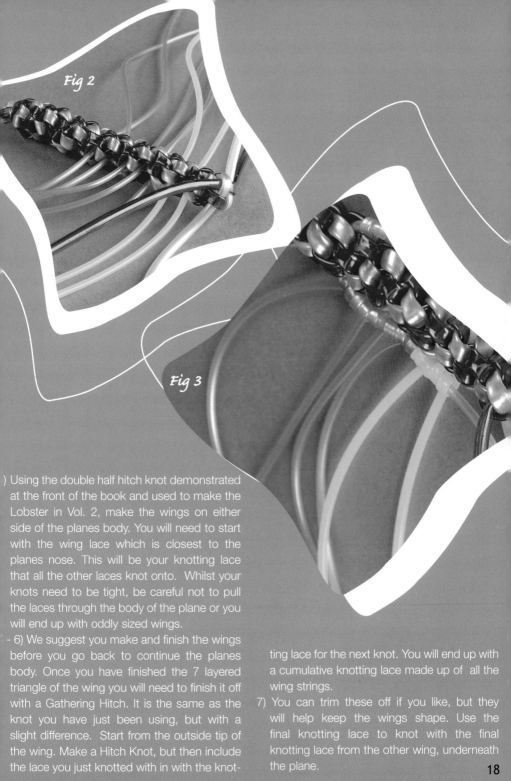

Fig 2

Fig 3

) Using the double half hitch knot demonstrated at the front of the book and used to make the Lobster in Vol. 2, make the wings on either side of the planes body. You will need to start with the wing lace which is closest to the planes nose. This will be your knotting lace that all the other laces knot onto. Whilst your knots need to be tight, be careful not to pull the laces through the body of the plane or you will end up with oddly sized wings.

- 6) We suggest you make and finish the wings before you go back to continue the planes body. Once you have finished the 7 layered triangle of the wing you will need to finish it off with a Gathering Hitch. It is the same as the knot you have just been using, but with a slight difference. Start from the outside tip of the wing. Make a Hitch Knot, but then include the lace you just knotted with in with the knot-

ting lace for the next knot. You will end up with a cumulative knotting lace made up of all the wing strings.

7) You can trim these off if you like, but they will help keep the wings shape. Use the final knotting lace to knot with the final knotting lace from the other wing, underneath the plane.

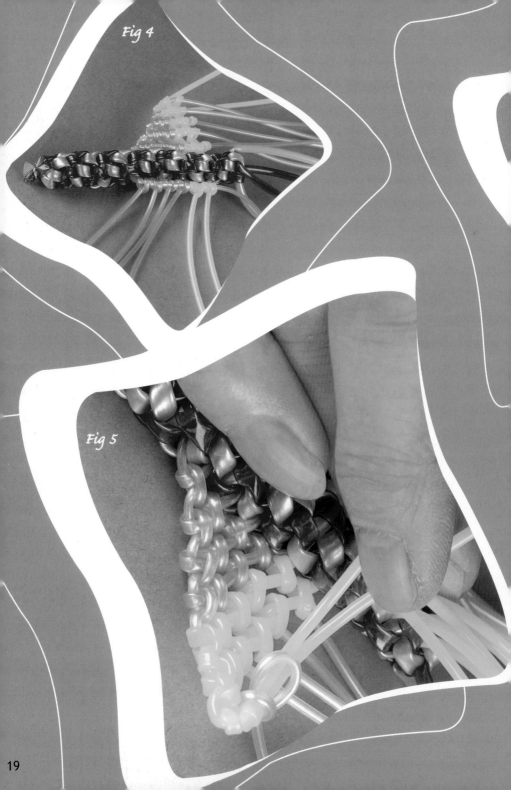

Fig 4

Fig 5

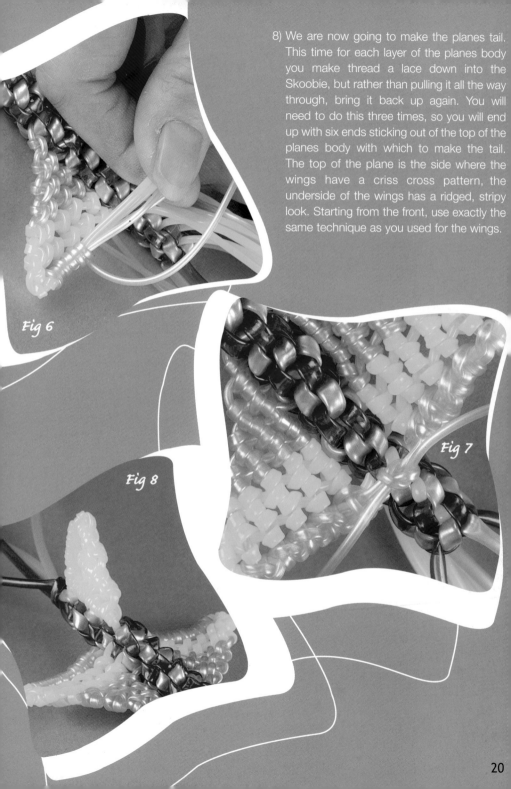

8) We are now going to make the planes tail. This time for each layer of the planes body you make thread a lace down into the Skoobie, but rather than pulling it all the way through, bring it back up again. You will need to do this three times, so you will end up with six ends sticking out of the top of the planes body with which to make the tail. The top of the plane is the side where the wings have a criss cross pattern, the underside of the wings has a ridged, stripy look. Starting from the front, use exactly the same technique as you used for the wings.

Fig 6

Fig 7

Fig 8

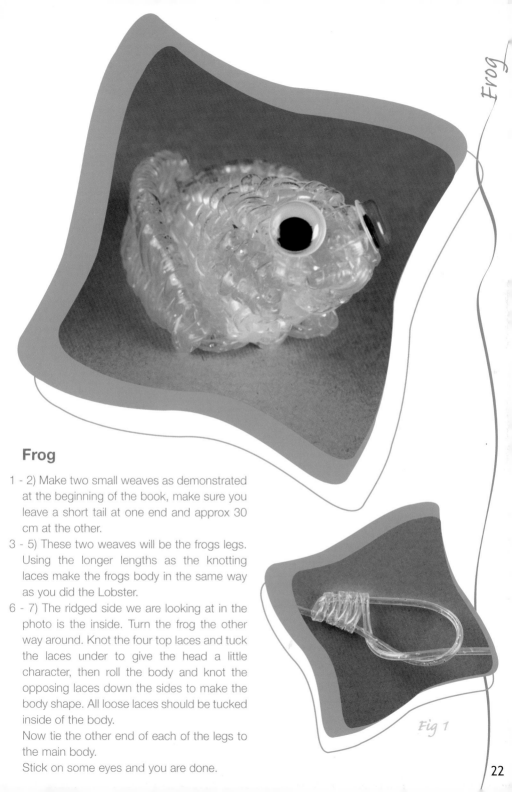

Frog

1 - 2) Make two small weaves as demonstrated at the beginning of the book, make sure you leave a short tail at one end and approx 30 cm at the other.

3 - 5) These two weaves will be the frogs legs. Using the longer lengths as the knotting laces make the frogs body in the same way as you did the Lobster.

6 - 7) The ridged side we are looking at in the photo is the inside. Turn the frog the other way around. Knot the four top laces and tuck the laces under to give the head a little character, then roll the body and knot the opposing laces down the sides to make the body shape. All loose laces should be tucked inside of the body.

Now tie the other end of each of the legs to the main body.

Stick on some eyes and you are done.

Fig 1

Fig 2

Fig 3

Fig 4

Fig 5

23

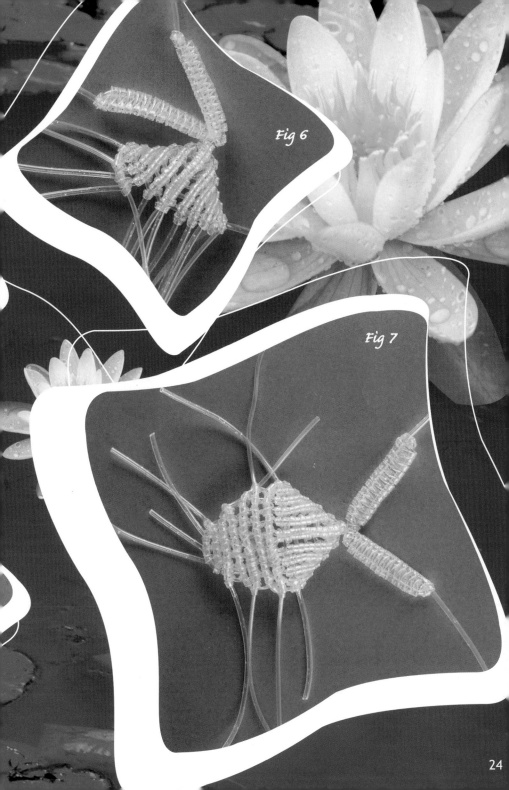

Fig 6

Fig 7

24

Snail

1) Make a loop with a large pipe cleaner. Cut a short length of lace and attach it to the loop using a Cow Hitch knot. This will be the antennae.

2 - 4) Tie a long lace between the antennae using the double half hitch, run it to the opposite end of the loop and attach in the same way. Then take it back up to the antennae again, thread it under one of the existing loops and start weaving.

Take a large pipe cleaner and spiral it to make the snails shell. You may find this easier if you wrap the pipe cleaner around a funnel to get a good shape.

Attach the shell to the snails back using some glue to hold it in place.

Fig 1

Fig 2

Fig 3

Fig 4

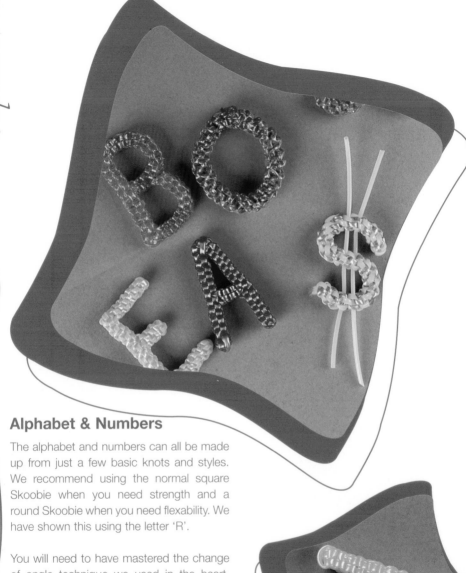

Alphabet & Numbers

The alphabet and numbers can all be made up from just a few basic knots and styles. We recommend using the normal square Skoobie when you need strength and a round Skoobie when you need flexability. We have shown this using the letter 'R'.

You will need to have mastered the change of angle technique we used in the heart. You will also need to be able to build your skoobies around pipe cleaners for extra strength and making shapes.

There are two types of curve. There are no strength problems with curves that join back onto themselves like B, D, 6 and 8. But letters like J and S and numbers like 5 and 3 need to be built onto pipe cleaners to help hold their shape.

Fig 1

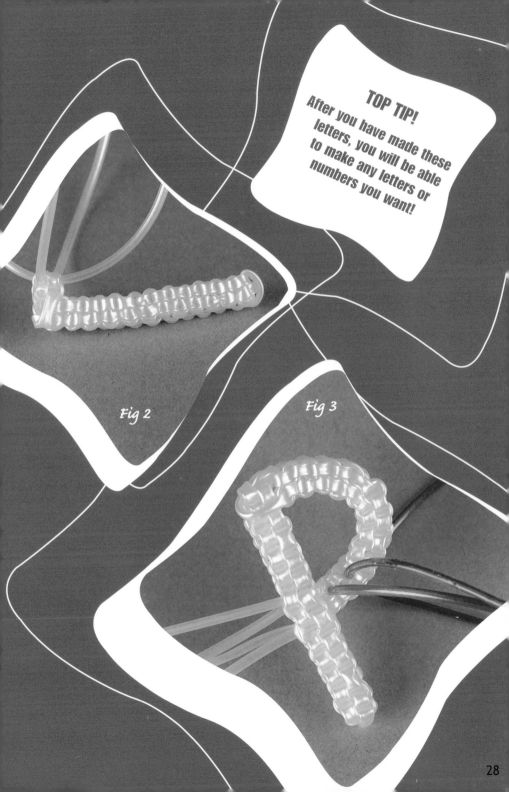

TOP TIP!
After you have made these letters, you will be able to make any letters or numbers you want!

Fig 2

Fig 3

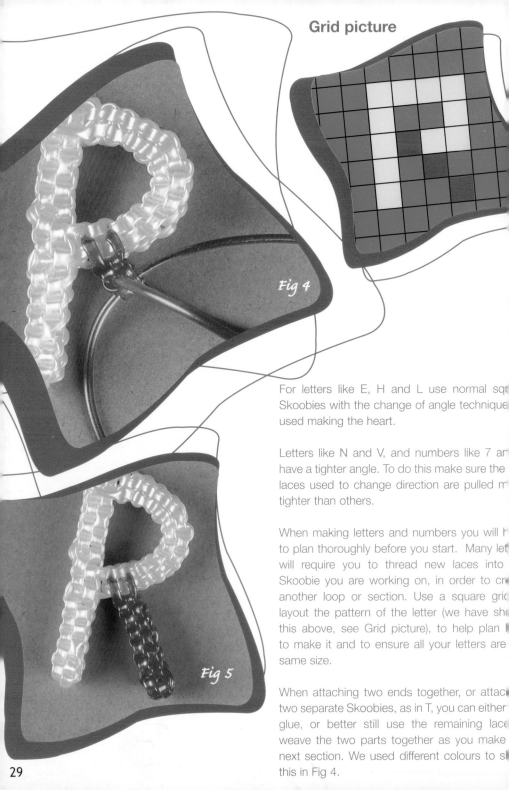

Grid picture

Fig 4

Fig 5

For letters like E, H and L use normal squ[e]
Skoobies with the change of angle technique
used making the heart.

Letters like N and V, and numbers like 7 an[d]
have a tighter angle. To do this make sure the
laces used to change direction are pulled m[ore]
tighter than others.

When making letters and numbers you will h[ave]
to plan thoroughly before you start. Many let[ters]
will require you to thread new laces into
Skoobie you are working on, in order to cr[eate]
another loop or section. Use a square gri[d to]
layout the pattern of the letter (we have sh[own]
this above, see Grid picture), to help plan [how]
to make it and to ensure all your letters are
same size.

When attaching two ends together, or attac[hing]
two separate Skoobies, as in T, you can either
glue, or better still use the remaining lace[to]
weave the two parts together as you make [the]
next section. We used different colours to s[how]
this in Fig 4.

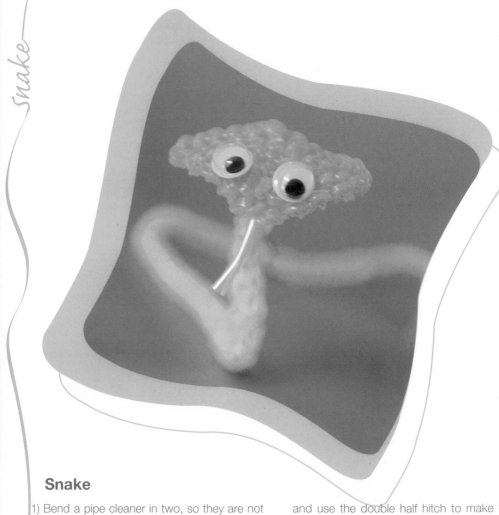

Snake

1) Bend a pipe cleaner in two, so they are not quite of equal length. This will help create the snakes tapering tail. Loop a lace with it, then use this and another lace to Skoobie around the pipe cleaner using a normal round Skoobie knot.

2) Skoobie until you have gone about 2 cm past the end of the pipe cleaner.
Continue to Skoobie with just 3 of the laces around the fourth lace for around 1cm, then cut off the remaining centre lace and continue to Skoobie a little longer. Then cut off another lace and knot the two remaining laces a little further. That completes the tail.

3) To make the head tie 6 cross laces directly above the top of the snakes Skoobied body,

and use the double half hitch to make th double half hitch triangle. Do this on bo sides. Taking the lace on the very outsic of the triangle for the knotting lace, kn the other way working back towards into th pipe cleaner. Repeat on both sides.
You should end up with six sets of lace which can be tied off against each other the top of the underside of the snakes no complete head.

4) There is a loop just under the snakes hea you could either tie a key ring to this, or yc can cut it and feed it through the head make a forked tongue. Stick some eyes c and go scare your friends.

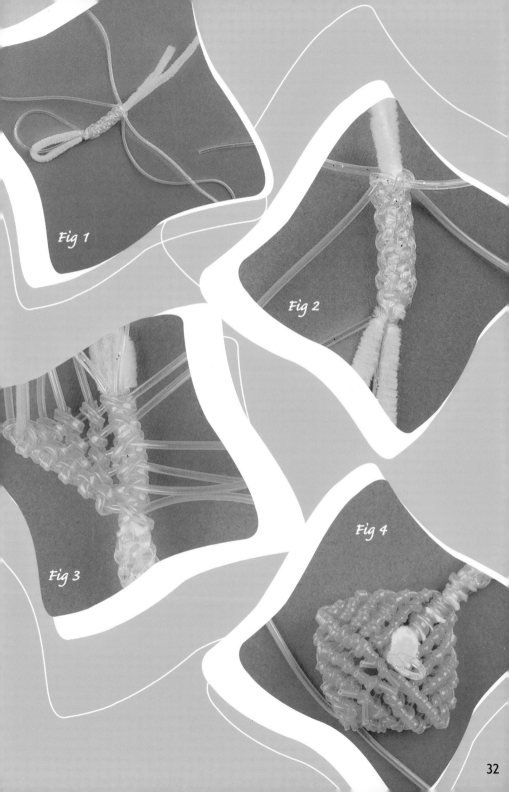

Fig 1

Fig 2

Fig 3

Fig 4

Here is an explanation for making the Lobster in Volume 2. If you couldn't work it out with just the pictures, try it again now you have the instructions as well. If you don't have Volume 2 you can find pictures of the Lobster on our website.

Take a blue lace, fold it in half, and knot at the mid point. These two blue laces will become the knotting laces that are central to all laces added.

Use a Double Half Hitch again, knot to attach one red lace to the blue laces. The red lace is looped twice around the blue laces to form this knot. Push this knot as close up to the blue knot as possible.

Repeat this 5 more times with new red laces.

Take the top red lace on the left side and using it as a knotting lace knot all the red laces down the left side with a clove hitch knot.

Take the next top red lace and repeat stage four. Keep repeating until all the red laces have been used as a knotting lace in turn. You will end up with a triangular shape.

Repeat on the other side.

Turn your lobster over and work from the other side for the next few stages.

Leave the furthermost red lace out as this will later form part of the claws.

The next outermost red lace (which run parallel to the blue Knotting laces) is your new Knotting lace. Use the clove hitch knot using all the strings (red and blue) from left to right.

10) At the right side leave the two red laces sticking out for claws later. Use the next red lace, which lies parallel to the blue laces and knot from right to left using all the laces (blue and red).

11) Turn the lobster back over again

12) Continue this process, never using the lace that has been left sticking out from the last row of knots, going right to left, then left to right in the following row, we will use this later when fininshing. The body should taper smaller and smaller.
The top three red laces on each side should be left for now. These will be plaited to make the claws

13) To make the tail, leave two loops of the blue laces sticking out, tie a knot at the end of them, leaving 5 cm to form the looped tail.

14) Using the remaining red laces give the body its shape by tying the laces in pairs across the underside of the body, tucking in loose strings as you go as well as the ends of the blue laces.

15) To make the claws, simply plait the three red laces we left on each side, and knot.

16) To make the antenna, knot a short piece of red lace around the blue lace at its nose and pull through the blue knot to make them face forward.

17) Stick on the eyes and give him a name.

My Skoobie Challenge

We have set you a new My Skoobie challenge! See if you are now clever enough to make these new My Skoobie creations! The answers will be revealed on our website. Use the special My Skoobie access code to find out!

It is amazing how many people My Skoobies appeal to. We have had emails from boys and girls between the ages of 5 to 85 and even beyond!

Good luck everybody!

These are
some of the
My Skoobie products
For more info go to
our website.

Your special My Skoobie
access code

UWINKING

www.ozbozz.co.uk

*Imagination
is only a
thought away ....*

Cool new My Skoobies Fashion Strings make a great accessory for every occasion, you can make friendship bands, keyrings, bracelets and loads more great stuff. My Skoobies come in transparent, neon, glitter and rainbow colours. Get them while they are hot!

This book will show you how to make some great accessories step-by-step.

Coming soon our brand new book **My Extreme Skoobies!**

FUNKY DIVA

My Extreme Skoobies
By Grossman

Check website for more details!

See our great range of My Skoobie Books

Published by H. Grossman Ltd.
www.ozbozz.co.uk

My Skoobies books are distributed and printed in the U.K. by H. Grossman Ltd, Herschel House, Quay Industrial Estate, Ashton Road, Rutherglen, Glasgow G73 1UB

UK £2.99 EUROPE €4.99

ISBN 0-9550407-3-6

9 780955 040733

Designed and produced by www.agi.co.uk

These books are also available French and German at **www.myskoobies.co**

LET THERE BE
LIGHT

**A veritable bible of behind the scenes
shenanigans and tittle tattle culled from five years
hard graft at Sunderland AFC**

Tony Gillan